SUPERHERO SMILES

by Jeni Donatelli Ihm

Eifrig Publishing LLC
Berlin Lemont

© 2020 by Jenifer D. Ihm
Photos © Nathaniel Edmunds Photography and Daniel Sonnentag

www.nathanieledmunds.com   www.theyhavenamesberlin.org @daniel_sonnentag

Additional photos were supplied by friends sharing their superhero smiles, including the author's and the publisher's children, folks at the Centre County Recycling and Refuse Authority, Trader Joe's, UPS, students celebrating their teachers in NY, and teachers and students coming together from the Chicago Public Schools, as well as Sandy Murgas Palermo, a recovered COVID-19 patient and nurse, and Michelle Johns Jordan, who is recovering from a severe case of the Coronavirus.

Printed in the United States of America

All rights reserved. This publication is protected by Copyright, and permission should be obtained from the publisher prior to any prohibited reproduction, storage in a retrieval system, or transmission in any form or by any means, electronic, mechanical, photocopying, recording, or likewise.

Published by Eifrig Publishing, PO Box 66, Lemont, PA 16851
Knobelsdorffstr. 44, 14059 Berlin, Germany

For information regarding permission, write to:
Rights and Permissions Department,
Eifrig Publishing, LLC
PO Box 66, Lemont, PA 16851, USA.
permissions@eifrigpublishing.com, 814.954.9445

Library of Congress Cataloging-in-Publication Data

Ihm, Jenifer D.
Superhero Smiles / written by Jenifer D. Ihm

p. cm.

Paperback: ISBN 978-1-63233-254-7
eBook: ISBN 978-1-63233-255-4

1. Juvenile Fiction-health. 2. Juvenile Fiction-emotions
I. Ihm, Jenifer D., Title.

24 23 22 21 2020
5 4 3 2 1

Printed on acid-free paper. ∞

Dedicated to all our unsung heroes
of the 2020 COVID-19 pandemic.
(Little hint-it's you)

Have you ever noticed when someone smiles at you,
it's hard not to smile back?
Sharing a smile can brighten a day
and make someone feel good.

Smiling at a friend who's sad might help them feel better faster than anything else possibly could. Smiling on the outside makes your insides smile too. Smile every chance you get; it might mend your blues.

Try skipping without smiling.

It's kinda hard, don't you think?

When you run and you play,
it will brighten your day.
And when you start smiling,
the joy starts multiplying.

Everyone has their own special smile to share. Go on and flash a smile, if you dare.

Turn the page and discover the wonderful world of superhero smiles.

We promise there will be no grimaces, sneers, or tiger snarls.

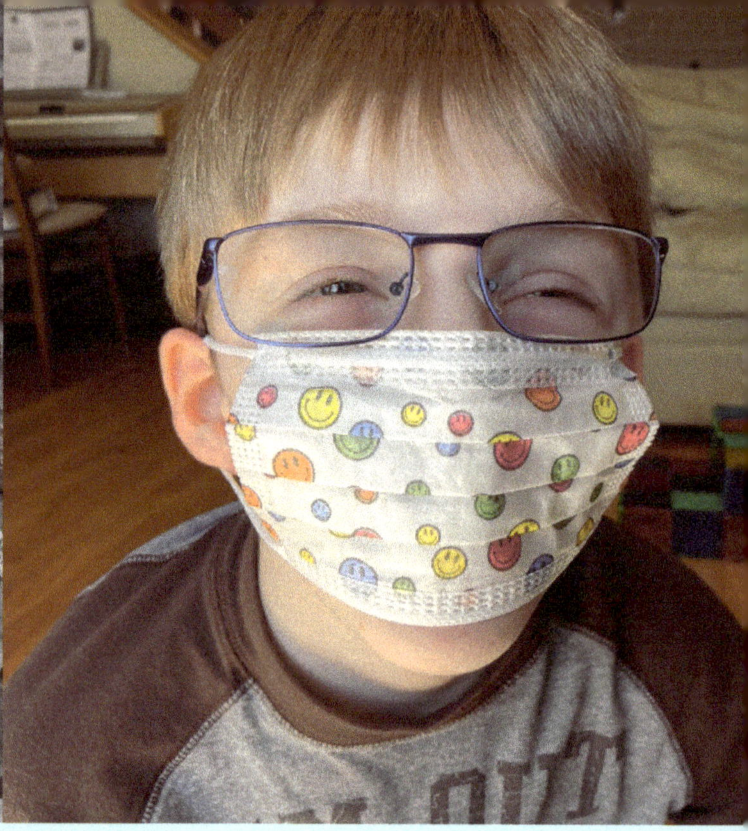

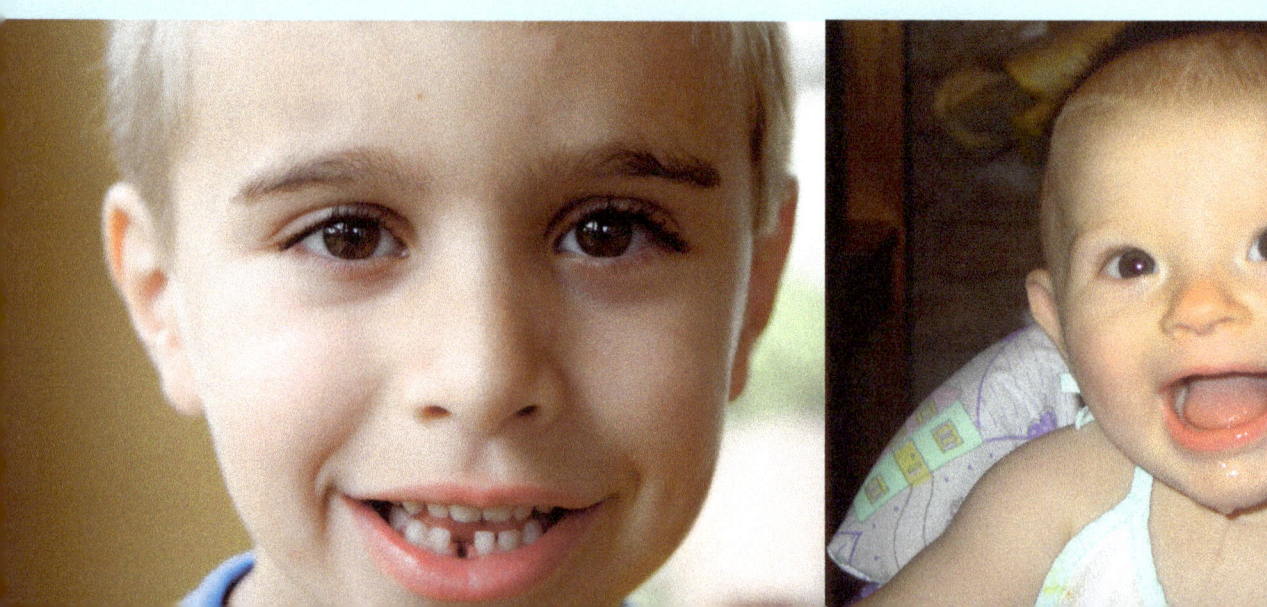

Some smiles are big and some are small.

Some show no teeth,
and some show them all.

Some smiles are wide and shimmer with braces.
Some folks like to smirk and make silly faces.

Smiles come from police officers, firefighters, nurses, doctors and medics, who bravely support us through this COVID-19 pandemic.

They all could use a little uplifting
so please share
a smile and a wave
as your way of gifting.

I CAN'T STAY HOME... I'M A HEALTHCARE WORKER!

Grandparents and babies share smiles over video chats, as new skills are learned and we wear silly hats!

We are all missing our playdates
and social connections,
so we find new ways to check in
with kindness and affection.

Some smiles have scars from a boo boo or cut, or babies born with a cleft lip and palate that the doctors carefully stitch up.

When you can't spend time with friends, special days can be tough.

But surprise drive-by birthdays will thrill you and shower you with love.

Our military women and men march on being heroic, while they continue to serve right through this pandemic.

...raduations and track meets
and dances and more
are off for the moment,
...ut will come back for sure.

We can celebrate remotely
...d share social media smiles
to keep our communities
connected yet safe,
as we must do for a while.

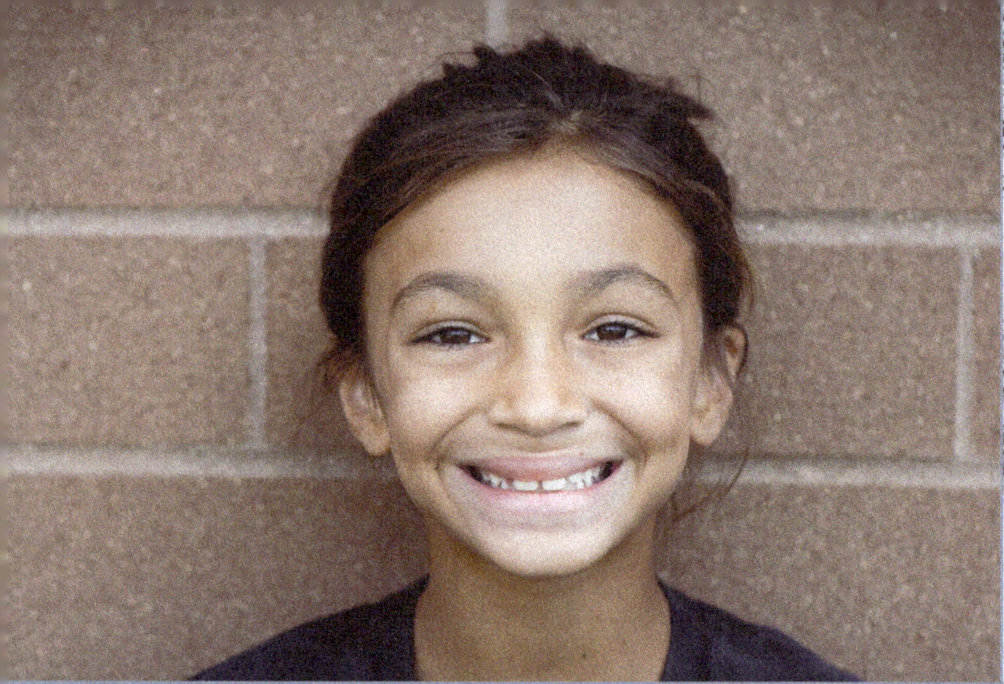

A jaw dropping smile brings energy to a room, which moms, dads and caregivers who are homeschooling will all need really soon.

Teachers make every effort to teach from a distance, using technology to keep kids learning with creative assistance.

Animals smile in all different ways. They like to act silly like you and me when we play, while keeping us company on these sometimes lonely days.

 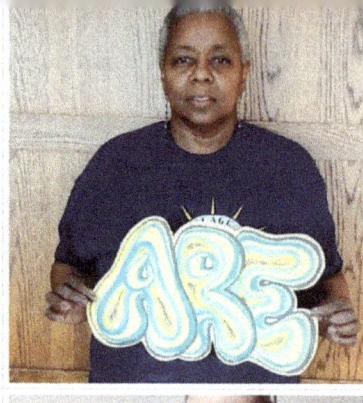  

Keep smiling and waving as you pass by your neighbor; social distancing, you see, is the new world order.

Smiles, too, are infectious and contagious to others. Everyone smiles, even sisters and brothers.

So spread some cheer and flash a smile,
and remember to deliver it
with superhero style!

Add your own Superhero Smile here!

www.ingramcontent.com/pod-product-compliance
Lightning Source LLC
Chambersburg PA
CBHW040011080526
44586CB00028B/2969